Incredible Plants!

Flowers, Leaves, and Other Plant Parts

Jacob Batchelor

Children's Press®
An Imprint of Scholastic Inc.

Content Consultant
Michael Freeling, PhD
Professor
Department of Plant & Microbial Biology
University of California, Berkeley
Berkeley, California

Library of Congress Cataloging-in-Publication Data
Names: Batchelor, Jacob, author.
Title: Flowers, leaves, and other plant parts / by Jacob Batchelor.
Description: New York, NY : Children's Press, an imprint of Scholastic Inc., 2020. | Series: A true book |
    Includes bibliographical references and index.
Identifiers: LCCN 2019004806 | ISBN 9780531234631 (library binding) | ISBN 9780531240069 (paperback)
Subjects: LCSH: Plant anatomy—Juvenile literature.
Classification: LCC QK641 .B375 2020 | DDC 571.3/2—dc23
LC record available at https://lccn.loc.gov/2019004806

All rights reserved. Published in 2020 by Children's Press, an imprint of Scholastic Inc.
Printed in Heshan, China 62

**Front cover: An avocado plant
growing from a seed**

**Back cover: A witch hazel plant
shooting out seeds**

Find the Truth!

Everything you are about to read is true *except* for one of the sentences on this page.

Which one is **TRUE**?

T or F   The needles on a cactus are a type of stem.

T or F   Some roots reach hundreds of feet into the ground.

Find the answers in this book.

3

Contents

The **BIG** Truth

Disappearing Forests

Loggers cut down billions of trees each year.

4

Hummingbirds drinking nectar

4 Looking at Leaves

5 Flowers and Fruits

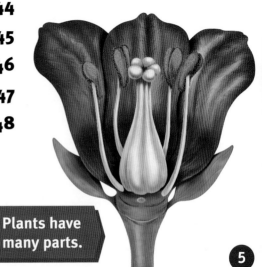

Plants have many parts.

5

Think About It!

Closely examine the photo on these two pages. Can you name some of the objects and organisms you see? Do you notice anything unusual or interesting about them? Is that bird about to fly away? Where did the hand come from? Gather evidence from the photo to support your ideas.

Intrigued?
Want to know more? Turn the page!

Artists prune a plant sculpture that is 50 feet (15 meters) tall.

If you guessed that the picture shows a sculpture made of plants, you were right! These sculptures were created for the Mosaiculture Festival in Montreal, Canada. The master gardeners who made the sculptures must understand every part of a plant to bring their creations to life. They pay attention to how the plants sprout from seeds, how big or strong their roots and stems will be, and what leaves, flowers, and fruits they will grow.

Together, these and all other plants on Earth make up the plant kingdom. Experts divide organisms into kingdoms, or groups. From the lowliest moss to the tallest giant sequoia tree, members of the plant kingdom share certain traits. Almost all plants make their own food by soaking up the sun. Most also have the same basic structures, or parts. This book will tell you all about what those parts are and how they fit together. Read on to find out more!

A chili pepper plant grows up and down.

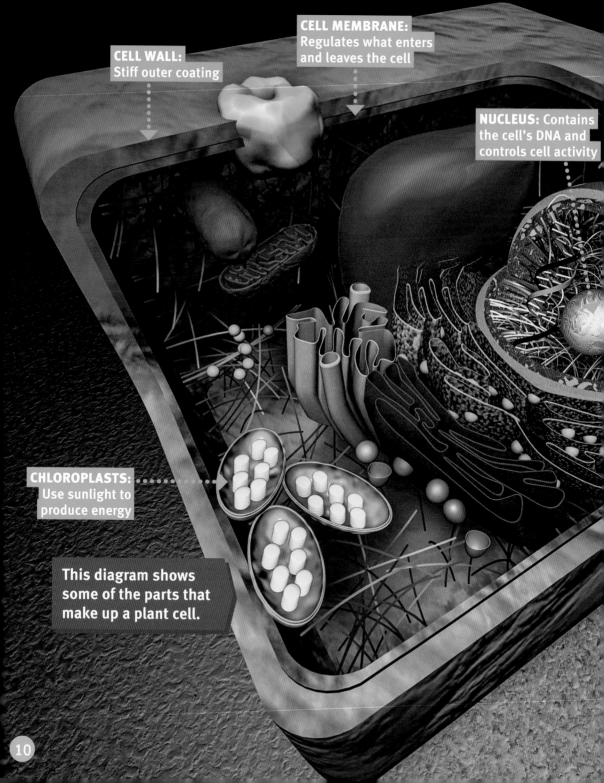

CELL WALL: Stiff outer coating

CELL MEMBRANE: Regulates what enters and leaves the cell

NUCLEUS: Contains the cell's DNA and controls cell activity

CHLOROPLASTS: Use sunlight to produce energy

This diagram shows some of the parts that make up a plant cell.

Inside a Cell

Plants are made up of many parts, from roots to leaves. But what are those parts made of? The answer is **cells**. A cell is the most basic unit of life. There are trillions of them in just you alone. Plants are also made up of many cells. Inside each cell are even smaller parts that serve different functions. Take a look!

Plant cells can be up to three times larger than animal cells!

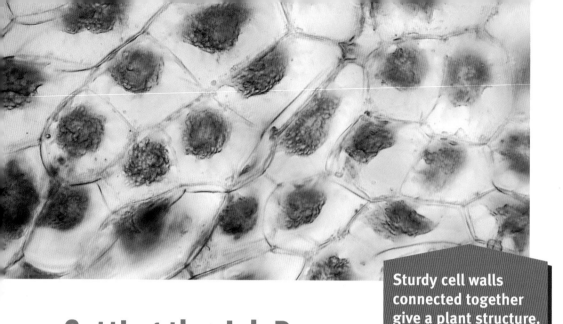

Sturdy cell walls connected together give a plant structure.

Getting the Job Done

If you could shrink and go inside a plant cell, what would you see? First, you'd have to get through the cell wall. This outer coating protects the cell and gives it structure. Luckily, the wall is slightly permeable. That means some materials, such as water, can pass through.

Next, you'd encounter the cell membrane. This layer inside the cell wall determines what comes in—and what goes out—of the cell. Head on in!

Inside the cell are several structures. Each one performs a special job. Green structures called chloroplasts catch energy from the sun and use it to produce food. There is also the **nucleus**. This is the brain, or control center, for the cell. It contains all the information and instructions needed for a cell to function.

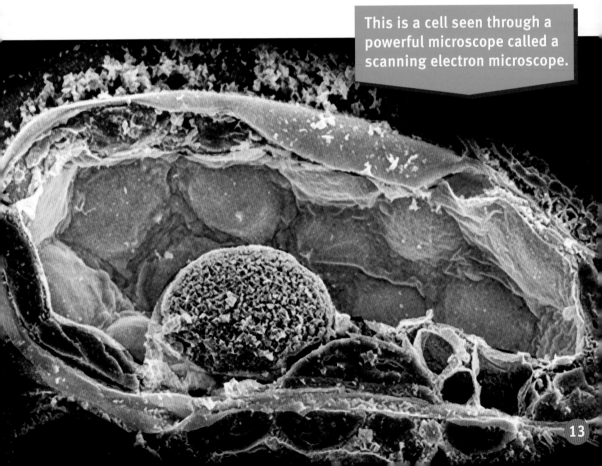

This is a cell seen through a powerful microscope called a scanning electron microscope.

It can take 20 kids stretched arm to arm to wrap around some sequoias.

A sequoia's seeds require fire to sprout!

Amazing Seeds!

The largest single tree in the world is a giant sequoia in California. It is nearly 100 feet (30 m) around at its base! About 2,000 years ago, this plant was just one of thousands of tiny seeds inside a pinecone. But one day, a fire ran through the forest. The resulting heat opened up the pinecone and released the seeds. One of those seeds **germinated** and began growing into the giant we see today.

Inside a Seed

Most of the world's plants are seed plants. They use seeds as one way to reproduce and grow. Although seeds come in every size, shape, and color, they all have similar structures that serve similar purposes. Many seeds, for example, have a hard shell called a seed coat. It keeps everything inside safe—sometimes for centuries!

Other plants, called gymnosperms, do not have seed coats. The giant sequoia is a gymnosperm. It releases "naked seeds" from its cones.

This plant was grown from a 30,000-year-old seed!

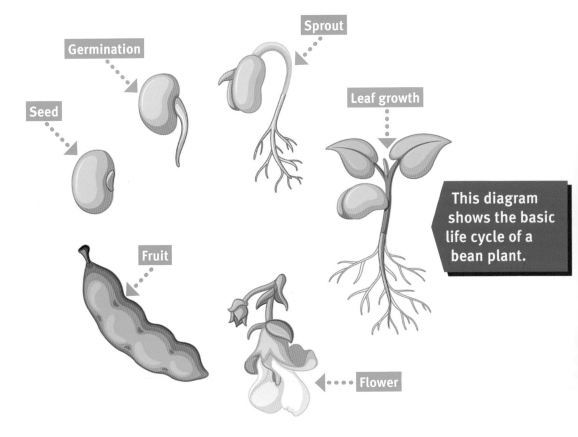

Seed

Germination

Sprout

Leaf growth

This diagram shows the basic life cycle of a bean plant.

Fruit

Flower

The most important part of a seed is its embryo. The embryo contains the cells of a young plant. The seed waits until it senses that the situation is perfect, with just the right amount of water and warmth. Then the embryo's cells begin to divide and multiply until the plant sprouts. The young plant can't make its own food right away. It relies on a store of extra food inside the seed.

Adapting to Grow

The goal of every plant is for its seeds to spread and grow into new healthy plants. But it's not always easy! Seeds often need to travel to just the right spot, where conditions are perfect for them to sprout. To accomplish that, plants developed ways that help seeds move to where they need to go and stay safe along the way.

Some plants, such as dandelions, create seeds that catch the wind and fly away. Other plants, such as palm trees, have seeds with tough shells that allow them to survive for years at sea. Animals help spread seeds by eating fruit. You can learn more about how that works on page 40.

Other plants don't have seeds at all. They release cells called **spores**. These grow into entirely new plants on their own.

This horsetail is releasing scores of spores.

The roots of a strangler fig can grow up to 15 feet (4.5 m) per year!

This fig tree grows over a temple at Angkor Wat in Cambodia.

Roots and Stems

Once a seed sprouts or a spore begins to grow, two of a plant's most important structures take over. One of those structures is the root system. Roots burrow down into the soil. They are responsible for anchoring the plant. Stems, on the other hand, do just the opposite. They reach up into the sky.

Roots Dig Down

Roots are good at their job. Just try to weed a garden! These tough plant parts spread out through the soil so they won't easily come out of the dirt. But roots have another important function. They collect water and nutrients. Threadlike structures called root hairs pull these life-giving substances from the soil. Then they funnel the materials up into the stems so a plant can grow.

Roots are so strong that they can break apart sidewalks.

Some roots, called taproots, extend deep into the earth. One wild fig tree in South Africa has a taproot reaching 400 feet (122 m) underground! **Fibrous** roots grow out far and wide. Oak tree roots, for example, can spread twice as far as the tree is tall. There are also roots that store a plant's food. This creates root vegetables such as carrots and beets. Other roots can even branch out and produce new plants. This is how bamboo forests grow.

This chicory plant has a long, strong taproot.

Stems Shoot Up

While the roots dig deep or wide, the stems grow up into the sky. Stems have the important function of carrying water and nutrients to various parts of the plants. They do this using special **tissue** made up of many cells. Phloem tissue carries the food and nutrients, and xylem tissue carries the water.

Plants can have two different types of stems: herbaceous and woody.

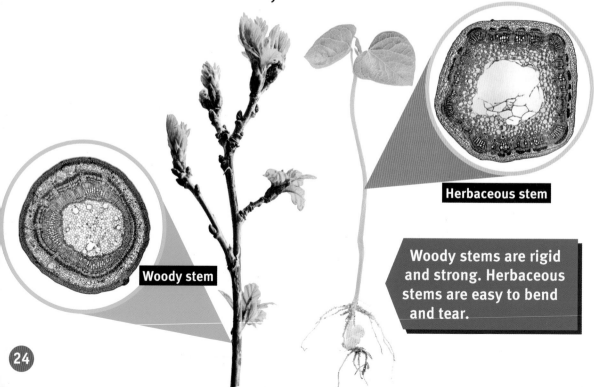

Herbaceous stem

Woody stem

Woody stems are rigid and strong. Herbaceous stems are easy to bend and tear.

If you've ever picked a daisy, you've come across an herbaceous stem. These stems are soft and easy to bend. Open one up and you'll feel the water inside. For some plants, having an herbaceous stem is particularly useful. Climbing

Vines can bend and reach to spread across walls and other structures.

vines grow and twist until they find something to latch onto. Then the stem curls around tightly before sending out another shoot. Other plants' stems turn so their flowers or leaves follow the sun.

Emerald ash borers can get under the bark of ash trees and cause serious damage.

Emerald ash borer

Not all stems are so fragile. Woody stems are hard and strong. Some are even resistant to fire! These stems grow an outer layer of bark. Bark protects the cells and tissues inside from disease and pests. Plants with woody stems include shrubs and trees. Some of these organisms can grow extremely tall. Redwood trees in California can reach nearly 400 feet (122 m)!

The Wood-Wide Web!

Trees may not have access to the internet, but they can still exchange information— and nutrients. Sometimes, the roots of different trees fuse together. This allows trees to share nutrients and water directly. But trees also use fungi called mycorrhizae to help their neighbors. Thick strands of these fungi form a dense network beneath the forest floor. Trees use the network to send resources to struggling saplings.

Disappearing Forests

Forests are among the world's most valuable resources. They are home to incredible numbers of species, including plants and animals that scientists have not even discovered yet. Forests also act as the planet's lungs. They inhale carbon dioxide from the air and exhale oxygen we can breathe.

Unfortunately, people have cut down much of the Earth's forests. This **deforestation** occurs for many reasons.

Logging

Loggers cut down trees to sell for building supplies and other uses. Experts estimate that the world lost an area of about 1,000 football fields each hour between 1990 and 2015.

Farming

People cut down forests to plant valuable crops such as palm oil trees. The world's palm oil plantations now cover an area the size of New Zealand.

Urbanization

As cities grow, forests are cleared to build more housing and businesses. No one knows how the world's forests will fare as the global population continues to grow.

An owl looks over its woodland home.

Many of the world's 10,000 bird species live in forests.

Looking at Leaves

Look up at a tree and what do you see? Leaves! Most plants couldn't survive without these structures. They absorb the sunlight needed for the plant to make food. Although almost all leaves have the same basic function, they come in many shapes and sizes. These different adaptations help plants survive in all kinds of environments.

Flowers bloom in the sunny hills of Switzerland.

Soaking in the Sun

Imagine the sun on your skin. Its warmth can feel nice, and it provides people with some important vitamins. Plants, though, use the sunlight to do even more. In fact, they use its energy to make food! This process is called **photosynthesis**. The chemical reaction benefits plants by providing them with food. It also benefits us by creating the oxygen we breathe.

Plants also breathe. They take in carbon dioxide through their leaves, and their roots absorb water. Energy from the sun causes the carbon dioxide to react with the water. The reaction creates sugar and oxygen. The plants use some of the oxygen to burn the sugar. As a result, the plants grow. Then the plants exhale the remaining oxygen.

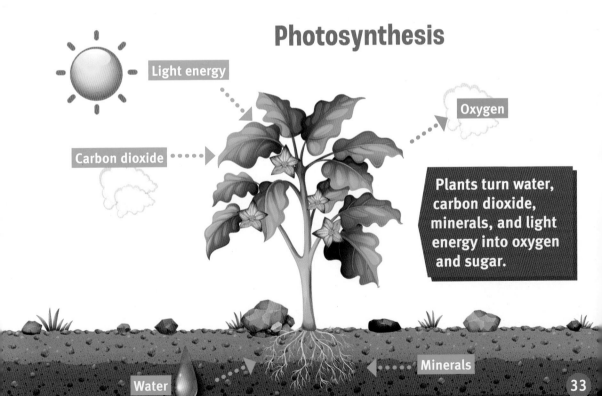

Photosynthesis

Light energy

Oxygen

Carbon dioxide

Plants turn water, carbon dioxide, minerals, and light energy into oxygen and sugar.

Minerals

Water

The Many Types of Leaves

A giant lily pad is a leaf. So are the needles on a cactus! Different kinds of plants have different leaf structures. Plants with broad, soft leaves capture a lot of sunlight. They lose water, however, through their stomata, the tiny holes through which gasses enter and exit the plant. Large-leafed plants tend to grow in wetter areas, where water is easy to find. Plants with narrow, waxy leaves don't catch a lot of sunlight, but they lose very little water. They tend to grow in dry areas.

Prickly pear cacti like this one have both long, stiff spines and tiny hair-like microscopic spines.

Space Plants!

Scientists are growing vegetables in Antarctica. The researchers are testing whether the plants can survive in conditions similar to those on the Moon or Mars. The vegetables need to withstand cold temperatures and photosynthesize without natural light. The plants are grown using a special LED light. They get nutrients from a liquid mixture instead of soil. Good news: The scientists say the veggies taste great!

A scientist inspects lettuce growing in a greenhouse designed for Mars.

Humans eat thousands of types of fruit!

Many markets and stores sell fruit from around the world.

Flowers and Fruits

Have you ever smelled a flower in full bloom? Or tasted a perfectly ripe fruit? Plants that produce flowers and fruits are called angiosperms. These plant parts are not just for show or to feed animals like us. Flowers and fruits allow plants to reproduce and spread their seeds to new places.

Pretty Useful

Birds, bees, and other **pollinators** feed on nectar. This is a sugary liquid deep inside a flower. But plants don't give away nectar for free. While pollinators eat, they rub against the flower's stamen. This is the male part of the plant. It gives off **pollen**, which is made up of a plant's male reproductive cells, or sperm.

Hummingbirds have long beaks that can reach nectar deep inside flowers.

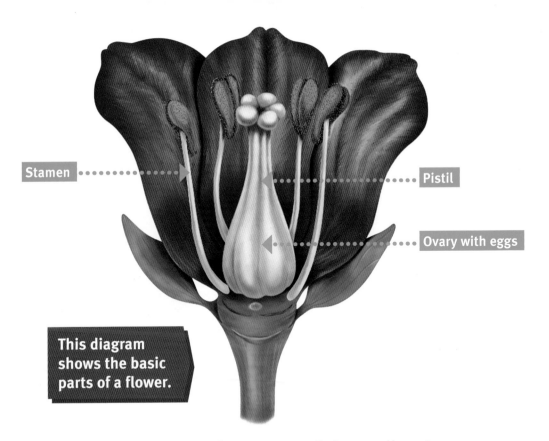

Stamen

Pistil

Ovary with eggs

This diagram shows the basic parts of a flower.

The pollinator rubs some of the pollen it collected onto a flower's pistil. This structure contains the female parts of the plant. The top of the pistil is sticky. It is perfect for picking up pollen. The pollen moves down into the pistil to where the plant keeps its egg cells. The cells in the pollen combine with, or fertilize, the cells to form seeds.

A dormouse has a snack of hawthorn berries.

Here Comes the Fruit!

Once one or more seeds are created, the female part of the plant surrounding them transforms into a fruit. A fruit contains much of the sugar the plant stores away from photosynthesis.

Did you know that it helps plants when animals eat their fruit? Fruits contain the plant's seeds. After an animal eats the fruit, it gets rid of the seeds in its droppings. This spreads the plant's seeds to new places.

From Seed to Fruit

Each plant part is important. Roots collect water. Stems carry water to the leaves. Leaves use water, air, and sunlight to produce sugar. Finally, the plant uses the sugar to create flowers, fruits, and other structures designed for reproduction. And then new plants grow. It's the circle of plant life!

You can help plants grow by planting seeds in your neighborhood.

Colorful Celery!

How is water carried through a plant? Learn more in this activity.

Materials

- 4 celery stalks
- Scissors
- 4 drinking glasses
- 4 different colors of food dye

Directions

snip

1 Use the scissors to snip off the bottom inch of the celery stalks.

2 Fill the glasses about halfway with plain water. Add a few drops of food dye to the water, using a different color in each glass.

3 Place a celery stalk in each glass. Let them soak for 20 to 30 minutes.

4 Look at the tops of the celery sticks. What do you see? (Tip: If nothing seems different, tear open the sticks and peel them apart!)

Explain It!

Using what you've learned in this book, can you explain what you see? If you need help, turn back to page 24.

True Statistics

Approximate number of plant species known to science: 400,000

Age of the oldest known tree, a bristlecone pine: More than 5,000 years

Growth rate of one kind of bamboo, the fastest-growing plant in the world: 35 in. (89 cm) per day

Height of the redwood tree Hyperion, the tallest tree in the world: 380 ft. (116 m)

Percent of plant species estimated to be threatened by extinction: 21

Diameter of the rafflesia flower, the largest flower in the world: 3 ft. (1 m)

Did you find the truth?

F The needles on a cactus are a type of stem.

T Some roots reach hundreds of feet into the ground.

Resources

Other books in this series:

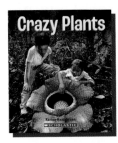

You can also look at:

Pipe, Jim. *You Wouldn't Want to Live Without Trees!* New York: Franklin Watts, 2017.

Spilsbury, Louise, and Richard Spilsbury. *Engineered by Nature: Killer Plants*. Minneapolis: Bellwether Media, Inc., 2017.

Willis, Kathy. *Botanicum*. Somerville, MA: BPP, 2017.

Glossary

cells (SELZ) the smallest units of an animal, plant, or other organism

deforestation (dee-for-is-TAY-shuhn) the removal or cutting down of forests

fibrous (FYE-bruhs) made up of fibers, or threadlike structures

germinated (JUR-muh-nate-id) sprouted, or put out shoots

nucleus (NOO-klee-uhs) the central part of a cell that contains all the information that determines how an organism looks and functions

photosynthesis (foh-toh-SIN-thuh-sus) a chemical process by which green plants make their food

pollen (PAH-luhn) the fertilizing particle of plants that consists of powdery, yellowish grains

pollinators (PAH-luh-nay-turz) organisms that transfer pollen between plants for fertilization

spores (SPORZ) plant cells that develop into a new plant

tissue (TISH-oo) mass of similar cells that form a particular part or organ of an animal or plant

Index

Page numbers in **bold** indicate illustrations.

About the Author

Jacob Batchelor studied English and creative writing at Dartmouth College in New Hampshire, and he currently writes and edits science-focused stories for Scholastic's *Science World* magazine. When he's not hanging out in the library or writing books for kids, he likes to take long walks in Prospect Park near his home in Brooklyn, New York.